CATS
GONE BAD

KAT SCRATCHING

amber
BOOKS

Published by
Amber Books Ltd
74–77 White Lion Street
London
N1 9PF
United Kingdom
www.amberbooks.co.uk
Appstore: itunes.com/apps/amberbooksltd
Facebook: www.facebook.com/amberbooks
Twitter: @amberbooks

ISBN: 978-1-78274-320-0

Project Editor: Sarah Uttridge
Designer: Keren Harragan
Picture Research: Terry Forshaw

Printed in China

Picture Credits
Alamy: 60 (Nurpoto.com)
Corbis: 62 (Thomas Peter/Reuters)
Depositphotos: 6 (Kuban Girl), 8 (Irin 717), 10 (Willeecole), 12 (James Steidl), 16 (Lady Lisa), 18 (Hanna Mariah),
22 (Pakhnyushchyy), 24 (Artem Povarov), 30 (Emmanuelle Bonzami), 32 (Eleonora Vatel), 36 (Tom Wang), 40
(Rommel Canlas), 44 (Kuban Girl), 46 (Art_Man), 50 (Alexy Trener), 54 (Plus 69), 56 left (Life on White), 58 (Mikhail
Olykainen), 64 (Andrejs Pidjass), 66 (Veda Gonzalez), 70 (Markus Gann), 74 (Jimboscar 7), 76 (Darzyhanna), 78 left
(Kipuxa), 78 top right (Taigi), 78 bottom right (VIP Design USA), 82 (Riderart), 82 left (Wavebreak Media), 84 right
(Photo Empire), 86 (Ok.Nazarenko), 88 left (Lovleah), 88 right (Andrey Kuzmin), 90 left & right (Wavebreak Media),
90 top centre (Mactrunk), 90 bottom centre (Karandaer), 94 top (Ronen), 94 bottom (Photo-Deti), 96 (Adogslifephoto)
Depositphotos/RasulovS: 14, 28, 34, 38, 42, 52, 68
Dreamstime: 20 (Xload)
Fotolia: 26 (Leoba), 72 (Anna Reich), 78 centre right (Pakpong Pongatichat)
Ingimage: 48, 56 right, 80
Istock: 92 (Shine 20)

Contents

Cool for Cats

"Yes, it's hot dogs for cool cats—I've climbed inside the fridge. And if you think that's unhygienic, you're right. I was ap-*paw*-lled at what I found. But I'm definitely cleaning up here. What's the wurst that could happen?"

Fridge Benefits

Photographs of cats snuggled inside refrigerators might look staged, but videos online show cats really opening fridge doors without any assistance. In the Czech Republic in 2012, a cat was filmed climbing up the handles of the fridge doors. It hung from the freezer door and propelled itself backward with enough force to swing the door open.

Feline Clean?

"I like to vacuum all over the house, on the Persian and the Oriental. I use it on the carpets and rugs, too."

Shaken and Furred

What does your cat get up to when it's home alone? In August 2010 in Bayreuth, Germany, neighbors called emergency services after hearing a cat screeching and a vacuum cleaner running for hours on end. When the fire-fighters broke into the apartment, they found the frightened cat quite safe and guessed that it had accidentally turned on the vacuum cleaner.

Cat Got Your Tongue?

"Who are you calling a hoodlum?"

Under House Arrest

A ginger cat in Rotherham, South Yorkshire, UK, was given an animal anti-social behavior order (ASBO) in 2014 after residents had complained that he was biting people, fighting with other cats, and refusing to leave people's homes. The court warned the owner that she would be charged with a crime if the cat went on to damage any property and asked her to keep him within the confines of her yard.

"I Tawt I Taw a Puddy Tat"

"They say that curiosity killed the cat, but that bird was as curious to fly outside the cage as I was to see what would happen if it did. That's all I'll say."

Watch the Birdie

Cats may show great patience in stalking birds, but how often do they catch them? Quite often, it seems. Cats, both domestic and feral, kill between 1.4 billion and 3.7 billion birds a year in the U.S., according to figures from the Smithsonian Conservation Biology Institute in Washington, D.C., in 2013.

Peeping Tom

"What am I going to see? *The Birds*, of course."

Catnip Popcorn

You buy your popcorn, find your seat, the lights go down, the movie begins. Well, not for all film felines. YouTube clips show cats who'll never know if the movie is the cat's pyjamas because they're too busy sniffing, playing with, and generally warming their faces on their bowls of popcorn. Some say that these days the movies are all about selling popcorn. Perhaps they're right.

Je Ne Regrette Chien

"Look at him with his silly scarf and name tag. Well, I can outstare him any day."

Cat Walks Dog

Dogs chase cats, right? But in the case of 2013 YouTube sensation "Cat Taking the Dog Home," it's clearly the cat who's boss. The cat, far smaller than the Jack Russell terrier, pulls the dog's leash and meows to keep the dog in check. That way, the cat leads the downtrodden dog, gives the leash a tug when the dog dawdles, and takes the dog up the stairs and home.

Who's Gonna Blink First?

"What's up? You've never seen a cat with a mustache before?"

Little Hitler, the Furry Führer

With a black toothbrush mustache and a severe side part, he is a cat that you might think one could only name "Adolf" or "Hitler." But Elena Suleymanyan, who lives in Moscow, calls her hairless Donskoy "Portos." Not that he can't be a little dictatorial; he'll only eat out of her hand or off a plate, turning his nose up at the cat bowl. "When his behavior is bad, I always say it's just the Hitler in him," explains Suleymanyan.

Cat Burglar

"If my owners had a TV, I wouldn't have to resort to this and look elsewhere. But how else am I going to watch *Dog Whisperer*?"

Playing Cat–ch Up

For two days in 2014, a cat terrorized a couple in their home in Kent, UK. Having climbed in to the house through an open window, the cat hid under a bed and sank its teeth and claws into Bruce Gough's arm when he tried to coax it out. The cat then caused havoc, breaking furniture but not leaving the property. Rescue came from a neighbor who donned his leather motorcycle outfit and a helmet before managing to wrap a blanket around the cat and release it outside the house.

Cat That Got the Cream

"Happiness is three things: A full belly, a warm carpet—
and knowing that tomorrow will be more of the same."

Something Fishy at the Airport

A cat found its way into Vladivostok International Airport
in Russia in December 2014 and proceeded directly to cat
heaven—the fresh fish counter in the airport's supermarket.
There, it climbed into the display case and gorged itself
on seafood, ruining $1000 worth of merchandise before a
customer spotted it. Rather than being punished, the cat was
adopted by Admiral Vladivostok hockey team.

Fat Cats

"You said you'd never in your lifetime see a cat on a banknote. Well, weren't you wrong?"

Fur Richer, fur Purrer

Cats love to roll in it—cash, that is. Website cashcats.biz invited owners to submit photos of their cats surrounded by trappings of their wealth. The response was immense, with photos of cats surrounded by cash and champagne flooding in. But not all cats were keeping their paws clean; some photos showed illegal drugs. As website owner Will Zweigart admitted, "I definitely get a lot of submissions from people who work in 'cash only industries,' if you will."

Cat in the Cockpit

"Whenever I have the chance to take a vacation, I pounce."

Domesticated Departures

When Mike Groleau was loading the baggage at Port Columbus Airport in Ohio in 2012, he thought he saw one of the suitcases move but dismissed the notion. Little did he know that a cat had, in fact, stowed away in the bag. The first Ethel Maze knew of it was when she opened her bags more than 900 miles (1448 km) later in Orlando and found her beloved Bob-bob had joined her on her week-long trip to Disney World.

Feline Southpaw

"And you thought only dogs could be boxers."

I Talk Cat—or Do I?

In 2015, Penny Adams of Nashville, Tennessee, bought an app to talk with her cat. Her high hopes were dashed, though, when one of the supposedly friendly sounds the app produced provoked the cat to scratch and snarl at her. It appears that the app does speak cat; we're just not sure what it's saying.

Hissing Fit

"They found my paw prints all over the crime scene."

When the Cat's Away

A missing cat is usually missed, but not Oscar, a Turkish Van living in Wingrave, Buckinghamshire, UK. His bites were so severe that one Wingrave resident had to spend six days in the hospital. Ironically, though, it was Oscar's bad behavior that brought him home again. He proved too difficult for his adoptive keepers to look after, so a vet found his microchip and traced Oscar's original owner. Although she was delighted to have him home, her neighbors armed themselves with water pistols.

Puss in Boots

"What did you expect—kitten heels?"

But Boots in Puss

In Brighton, UK, in 2015, a cat named Garry was taken to the vet for a routine vaccination. The vet, however, discovered a mass in his stomach. The vet suspected that it was a tumor and told his owner to prepare for the worst. Further investigation, however, revealed that Garry had eaten numerous shoelaces and hair bands. After surgery to remove these, he made a full recovery, while his owner kept any loose shoelaces out of reach.

Champion Dribbler

"It wasn't until I saw Luis Suarez play soccer that I realized how good I'd be at it—I can bite better than he can."

Turfed Out

What can upstage 22 top soccer players during a match? Yes, a black cat, choosing to pad out on to the field. This happened in August 2014 in a Spanish league match between Barcelona and Elche at Barcelona's Camp Nou stadium. Moving like a true Cat-alan, the cat dodged a few players before being chased off the field by an official. Barcelona won 3–0.

Strong Arm of the Paw

"I wasn't fouling; I was just marking territory."

I've Been Collared

Guards at a prison in Moldova in 2013 were used to seeing a grey and white cat walk in and out of the prison grounds. But one day, something caught their eye—the cat was wearing a peculiar collar. Stopping the cat, they found that the collar contained two bags of marijuana. The guards suspected that someone in a nearby village was using the cat as a drug mule and began a search for its trainer.

Sour Puss

"Do you want me to drag my claws down the blackboard again? No? Well then, repeat after me: 'The owl and the pussycat ...'"

Don't Smile for the Camera

Smile and the world smiles with you, but not so for internet sensation Grumpy Cat. Her miserable mien has been the making of her, earning her $100 million through books, merchandise, endorsements, and a movie. Within days of uploading a video of Grumpy Cat to YouTube, her owner Tabatha Bundesen from Morristown, Arizona, was able to give up her waitressing job and dedicate herself to the cat's career.

I Drive a Catillac

"This driving is making me hungry, can we stop off for a burger and some pet-atoes?"

Cat Pit-stop

A 70-year-old woman was driving her car with her cat in Folsom, California, in 2008, when the cat attacked her face. The woman lost control of her Toyota Solara and plowed into the wall of a Barbecue Express diner. She injured two diners who were hit by a piece of wall, a soft drink machine, and a table. It's not reported whether they took home a doggy bag.

I Can't Stand Poochini

"Favorite singer? Cat Stevens."

Vinyl Attraction

"Is this love?" sang Bob Marley on the record player. Perhaps it was, even at first sight, for two-year-old Furby when she saw the turntable in use. Intrigued by the rotating disc in the home of James Corballis in Galway, Ireland, she pressed her paw onto the record, speeding it up, slowing it down—doing a little "scratching," in fact. But like all true fans, she just couldn't get enough and jumped onto the turntable, only to find herself trapped, spinning around until Corballis rescued her.

In The Pet-itentiary

"I've got a nine-lives sentence."

Mr. Smuggles

Cats wandering in and out of prison gates might seem innocent enough. At Romero Nobrega prison in Brazil in 2015, however, guards discovered that cats were being used to smuggle in goods strapped to their bellies. They found one cat that appeared to be wearing a coat carrying four cell phones, chargers, and sim cards.

*Cat*ankerous

"Look, it's a selfie, OK? They always make faces a bit scary."

Cat Chases Bear up Tree

You might imagine that if a black bear confronted a cat, the feline would be the frightened one. But this wasn't the case when a black bear wandered into a yard in New Jersey in 2006 and came face to face with Jack, a tabby. Although clawless, Jack was territorial about the yard and chased the bear up a tree. He kept the bear clinging to the branches for 15 minutes before his owner took him inside, allowing the bear to climb down and slink off back into the woods.

Wetter Than a Catfish

"You think I look bad? You should see the other cat."

Catty Behavior

In a popular YouTube clip, one cat watches from the side of a swimming pool while another struggles in the water. When the swimming cat reaches the top of the ladder, the mean cat pushes it back into the water. But when the wet cat climbs the ladder for a second time, it has learned its lesson. It stops just below the top. The other cat still lashes out, but, with nothing to hit, loses its balance and falls into the water.

Domesticated Disturbance

"Do you think I'm looking out for a burglar? An intruder? No, your home has already been invaded—by me! I'm eating your food, sleeping on your bed, making you work for ME."

Pet Holds Family Hostage

In 2014, a couple with a baby in Portland, Oregon, were forced to call the police after their cat cornered them in one of their bedrooms. The incident began when the cat scratched the baby, and the baby's father kicked it. After that, the cat attacked the family, biting them and lashing out if they tried to pass it. Eventually, the police caught the pet with a snare and freed the family.

51

Paw Us Another One

"From the glasses and hat, you might have expected that I was a German Rex, but I'm a Birman. Geddit? *Beer*man."

Squatters' Rights

When a cat began appearing every day at the Blunsdon Arms pub in Swindon, Wiltshire, UK, in 2008, customers would give it scraps of their lunch. But that's where the problems began: because the pub served food, health and safety laws meant the cat wasn't allowed inside. So, a notice was put up announcing that the cat was barred from the pub. Unsurprisingly, the cat ignored this. Not only that, it was very territorial and would stare down other cats if they tried to enter.

Cat with Added Byte

"I admit it does look a little unusual for a mouse, but I'm going to eat it anyway."

Inspecting the Gadgets

A study has calculated that between 2010 and 2015, pet cats and dogs caused $2.36 billion worth of damage to laptops, tablets, and cell phones in Europe. Britain suffered the worst, with most incidents the result of a cat or dog mistaking the device for a chew toy, knocking the gadget off surfaces, stepping on them, or spilling things on them.

Cat and Mouse

"Me? I wouldn't hurt a fly ... A mouse, though, is another matter altogether."

Mouse Catcher in a Jam

A cat chasing a mouse got its head caught in a jar in which the mouse was hiding. The tabby, called Mindy, was seen wandering down a road in Peterborough, UK, in January 2007, with the jar stuck to its head and the mouse inside—an inch from the cat's mouth. A motorist took the cat to a police station, but they were unable to pry the jar off the cat's head. Finally, Mindy smashed the jar on the floor, releasing herself and leaving the mouse to escape unharmed.

Survival Kit

"Hey, I'm looking at you... well, get some blinds then if that bothers you."

Window Pain

It was nearly curtains for two cats in Sichuan Province, China, in 2015 when they became trapped between the panes of a double-glazed window. While initially the cats seemed comfortably snug, they risked suffocation in the enclosed space. A passerby noticed the cats' dilemma, but the only way to rescue them was to dig a hole in the wall beneath the window and drag the cats out. They weren't happy.

Cat That Got the Green

"What are you talking about? Of course green is a cool color. The Hulk, Yoda, Shrek—all cool cats."

All Cats Are Gray in the Dark

When residents in Varna, Bulgaria, spotted a luminous green cat in 2014, they were perplexed about the cause of its unusual coloring. Was it toxic? The result of genetic engineering? Or simply the most envious cat ever seen? Investigations, however, revealed that the cat simply liked sleeping in a pile of green paint. And if his friends were envious, they didn't show it in the color of their coats.

Cats Watch *The Mousetrap*

These cats *purr*port to be wild—even the one wearing a collar.

Cat Island

Aoshima Island in Japan is only one mile (1.6 km) long but is home to 120 feral cats. Now outnumbering the island's handful of humans six to one, the cats were introduced to Aoshima to deal with mice that plagued fishermen's boats. They stayed on—and multiplied. Aoshima is now known as "Cat Island" and receives visitors who come just to see the feral felines.

Cats Will Fly

"I'm much more comfortable in the air than the water, but then I would say that, I'm a Libran—It's an air sign."

Cat Falls Prey to Gravity

If cats have nine lives, Martin, a cat in St. Petersburg, Florida, might have used them all at once in 2009 when he fell from a ninth-floor condominium to the street below. He didn't even land on his feet. Falling, instead, on his face, he broke some teeth and suffered internal bleeding. "I've told him cats don't fly," said Martin's owner, Dr. Bob Wallace, "so we have to convince him now that he's a totally indoor cat." Martin is no longer allowed on the balcony.

Cat Denies Fatsuit

"Fat? No. Perhaps a whisker overweight. But it has its benefits; skinny cats can't sit like this."

Flabby Tabbies

Cats are now so fat that diabetes clinics are opening for them. British cats are on average 25 percent heavier than they were ten years ago. The causes of their weight increase and diabetes are—surprise, surprise—lack of exercise from living inside and poor diet. Not only can their increased weight lead to liver problems and arthritis, it can also cause skin problems because the cats can't stretch enough to groom themselves properly.

I Spy, with My Cat's Eye ...

"I'm just using these binoculars to try to look normal. The truth is, my eyes really are this big."

A Tail of Antennae

During the Cold War, the CIA spent what's believed to have been millions of dollars on a project trying to use cats as listening devices. However, for all their technical wizardry in implanting batteries in cats and using their tails as antennae, the CIA failed to grasp one basic thing about cats: the only training they'll accept is housebreaking. Instead of eavesdropping on the conversations of Soviet agents, the cats would wander off and find something more interesting to do.

Meow-ow-ow

"Not only did they declaw me, they took my mojo, too, if you know what I mean. I feel so ... so ... Actually after that operation, I don't feel very much anymore."

Cat from the Dead

What's worse than your cat dying? Perhaps burying it, grieving, and then having it reappear on your doorstep. That's what happened to Ellis Hutson in Tampa, Florida, in 2015, when a car knocked down his pet cat, Bart, and the vet declared Bart dead. The cat was buried, but five days later, the injured feline reappeared at Hutson's home. It's believed that Bart regained consciousness underground, dug his way out, and then lay low for a few days before making his way home.

Is Your Engine Purring?

"If you call me dipstick again I'll blow a gasket!"

Catalytically Converted

On sunny days, cats enjoy lounging on the hood of a car. On chilly mornings, however, the warmest place for a cat is curled around the engine. On the 60-mile (97 km) journey from Belfast to Derry in Northern Ireland in the winter of 2012, Gary O'Sullivan noticed a strange noise coming from the engine. Only on reaching Derry did he look under the hood and find that a stowaway tabby had climbed in around the engine. The cat was a little shaken but unharmed.

Cat Barks Up Wrong Tree

"Look, while you're climbing up to rescue me, I'll pussyfoot around for a while and then jump down on my own, OK?"

A Pawtionary tail

Carrie Courtney of Hoddesdon, Hertfordshire, UK, climbed a tree in her yard in 2014 in an effort to rescue her cat—and got stuck herself. Not only was the cat still out of reach, but Courtney found that she'd climbed too high to climb back down. Much to her embarrassment, her family had to call the fire department, who used the ladders to free Courtney and her cat. The fire department's advice was, when a cat appears stuck up a tree, nine times of ten, it'll find its own way down.

Precious Puss

"Diamonds and cats are the *purr*fect combination because they're absolute opposites: diamonds don't scratch."

CAT Scan Reveals Taste for Diamonds

"Never leave your valuables unguarded—even at home," might be the moral Steve Digby and Francine Lace of Wythenshawe, Manchester, UK, learnt when Francine's diamond and opal pendant disappeared from their coffee table. Unable to find the item, they suspected that their cat Oliver was the culprit—after all, the pendant had been lying next to Oliver's treats. An X-ray revealed the pendant, complete with 24–inch (61 cm) chain, lying in Oliver's stomach. It was safely removed during surgery and is now kept out of paws' reach.

Paws For Thought

"Talk about ungrateful! If I hadn't set the house on fire, they'd never have redecorated that kitchen."

Cat on a Hot Tin Loaf

A cover designed to protect toasters instead contributed to a fire in Port Townsend, Washington, in 2010. The owner's cat, Osiris O'Malley, had been sleeping on top of the protective cover on the toaster. During the night, however, Osiris pressed the toaster lever, activating it and setting the cover on fire. Flames reached the cabinets. The homeowner awoke to find her kitchen on fire. Osiris and the owner escaped unharmed, but the damage was estimated to cost $5000 to repair.

Caterwalling

"Well, if you won't install a cat flap I'll just have to make one myself, won't I?"

Marv's Marvellous Recovery

Curiosity may well have got the better of a cat called Marv in Bristol, UK, in 2015, when he managed to wedge himself upside down in a 5-inch (12.7 cm) gap between two garage walls. His neighbor first noticed meowing apparently coming from the wall. Unable to coax him out, his owner called the fire department, who had to chisel away a cinder block in the wall so that the cat could be dragged out backwards.

Puss is Put on Parole

"They've threatened to put me in the doghouse again."

"Rescue Me from My Rescue Cat!"

In 2008, Theo Morgan and his wife rescued a cat called Eric from Battersea Dogs & Cats Home in London. Two years later, Theo asked his vet whether he would put Eric down—not to end Eric's misery, but Theo's. Eric, who had a metal back leg after being hit by a car, shied away from any affection. However, he screeched all night, ripped off wallpaper, tore up furniture, and terrorized the neighbors and their cats until they moved away. After expensive surgery on Eric's leg, a despairing Theo wondered if it was time to put the cat to sleep. He didn't, instead giving Eric one last chance.

Cat Power

"If I was supposed to speak human, it would have happened by now."

Feline Intuition

If you've ever wondered whether your cat doesn't recognize you or is simply ignoring your command, research has found the answer: you're being given the cold shoulder. In 2013, scientists at the University of Tokyo studied 20 cats, monitoring their movements, vocalization, and eye dilation in response to recordings of strangers or owners calling their names. The responses showed that they could identify their owners, but that wasn't going to make them budge.

Raising Canine

"I'm not screeching or shrieking, yowling or wailing, howling or bawling. I'm caterwauling."

Feline Phenomenon

Bluey loves to purr, but she does it so much of the time and at such a volume that it put potential owners off picking her at her pet rehoming center in Cambridge, UK, in 2015. Tests show that Bluey's purrs can reach 93 decibels—louder than a passing train and four times louder than an average cat. It's also possible that the 12-year-old is a little hard of hearing. Undeniably loud and perhaps a little deaf though Bluey may be, she did eventually find a new owner.

Not To Be Sniffed At

"Some pusses go scent-imental over strong aromas."

Ow de Toilette

In 2014, Ian Olver of Plymouth, UK, put on a splash of Hugo Boss Bottled Night aftershave before going to visit his neighbors. But unknown to Olver, his neighbor's cat, Blue, had a phobia about strong scents. No sooner was Olver through the door than Blue leaped at him, landing on his head. He managed to fight Blue off, but the three-inch (7.6 cm) gash on the back of his head required stitches. Animal psychologist Dr. Roger Mugford said that Blue may have perceived the smell of the aftershave as a threat.

One Puss, Two Bags of Cats

"Now, if I've followed this correctly, these two are arguing about who gets to look after me. Truth is, it's all the same to me. As long as they feed me, I don't really care who they are."

A Pawcity of Cats

The Alexanders named him Ming because he liked to mingle so much. Perhaps too much, because Ming's periods of absence, during which he always lost his collar, kept increasing until, one day in 2010, he didn't return at all. For four years, the family in Wellington, New Zealand, didn't see Ming—and then he reappeared. It transpired that another family, the Lees, had assumed he was a stray because he spent so much time with them. They'd moved away, taking him with them. Now, however, they were back in the Alexanders' neighborhood. His return, though, created a problem: Whose cat was he now?

Thieving Tom

"Me? Bad? Butter wouldn't melt on my paws."

Brazen Bra Snatcher

Dusty, a cat in San Mateo, California, has stolen so many items from neighbors that his owners staged a reverse garage sale, inviting people to reclaim their stolen goods. It has even been suggested that he's suffering from a form of obsessive-compulsive disorder. He is so thorough that when he stole a tennis shoe, he returned to pick up its partner, and he made two trips to collect both pieces of a bikini.

Subway Surfers

"When we heard about the Brooklyn Flea market, we knew that was the place for us. And what better way to get there than via the subway. After all, isn't it a little like modern-day *cat*acombs?"

Mancattan Transfer

Some people might be good-looking enough to stop traffic, but two kittens in New York managed to stop two lines on the subway in 2013. The eight-week-old kittens were spotted on tracks in Brooklyn, causing an outage on the B and Q lines while NYPD officers searched for them. Commuters' journeys were disrupted for several hours before the cats were caught. They were subsequently taken to an animal shelter.